Amazing Animals

Bears

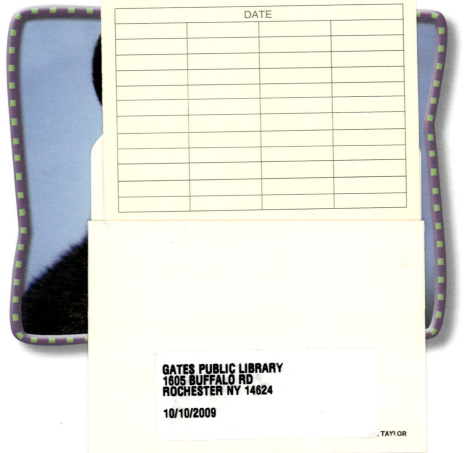

DATE			

Please visit our web site at www.garethstevens.com
For a free catalog describing our list of high-quality books, call 1-800-542-2595 (USA) or 1-800-387-3178 (Canada).
Our fax: 1-877-542-2596

Library of Congress Cataloging-in-Publication Data

Lukas, Catherine.
   Bears / by Catherine Lukas.
        p. cm.—(Amazing animals)
     Previously published: Pleasantville, NY: Reader's Digest Young Families, c2005.
     Includes bibliographical references and index.
     ISBN-10: 0-8368-9104-X   ISBN-13: 978-0-8368-9104-1 (lib. bdg.)
     ISBN-10: 1-4339-2021-2   ISBN-13: 978-1-4339-2021-9 (soft cover)
   1. Bears—Juvenile literature. I. Title.
   QL737.C27L85 2009
   599.78—dc22   2008027899

This edition first published in 2009 by
Gareth Stevens Publishing
A Weekly Reader® Company
1 Reader's Digest Road
Pleasantville, NY 10570-7000 USA

This edition copyright © 2009 by Gareth Stevens, Inc. Original edition copyright © 2005 by Reader's Digest Young Families,
Pleasantville, NY 10570

Gareth Stevens Senior Managing Editor: Lisa M. Herrington
Gareth Stevens Creative Director: Lisa Donovan
Gareth Stevens Art Director: Ken Crossland
Gareth Stevens Associate Editor: Amanda Hudson
Gareth Stevens Publisher: Keith Garton

Consultant: Robert E. Budliger (Retired), NY State Department of Environmental Conservation

Photo Credits
Front cover: PhotoDisc, Inc., title page: Dynamic Graphics, Inc., contents page: Dynamic Graphics, Inc., pages 6-7: Dynamic Graphics, Inc., pages 8-9: Dynamic Graphics, Inc., page 11: Digital Vision, page 12: Corel Professional Photos, page 13: Nova Development Corporation, pages 14-15: Dynamic Graphics, Inc., page 16: Daniel Cox/Corbis, page 18 (lower left): Corel Professional Photos, pages 18-19: Dynamic Graphics, Inc., pages 20-21: Dynamic Graphics, Inc., page 22: Corel Professional Photos, pages 24-25: Dynamic Graphics, Inc., page 26: Corbis Corporation, page 29: Dynamic Graphics, Inc., page 30: image100 ltd., pages 32-33: PhotoDisc, Inc., page 34: Corel Professional Photos, page 35: Corel Professional Photos, page 37: Digital Vision, pages 38-39: Dynamic Graphics, Inc., page 40 (top, bottom): Dynamic Graphics, Inc., page 41: Digital Vision, page 43: Brand X Pictures, pages 44-45: Dynamic Graphics, Inc., back cover: Dynamic Graphics, Inc.

Printed in the United States of America

1 2 3 4 5 6 7 8 9 13 12 11 10 09

Amazing Animals
Bears

By Catherine Lukas

Gareth Stevens
Publishing

Contents

Chapter 1
A Bear Cub Grows Up

Sweet Tooth

Black bears like to lick the sweet sap found under the outer layer of tree bark. The bears strip away the bark to get to the sapwood.

On a winter night inside her **den**, a mother bear gives birth. Her **cub** is as tiny as a kitten and has hardly any fur! He nuzzles against his mother and drinks her warm milk.

For two months, snow falls outside. While the mother bear sleeps, her baby drinks, sleeps, and grows. After four weeks, his eyes open. He is now covered with fur.

One day the bears wake up to a dripping sound. The snow is melting. The cub sniffs the warm spring air. Then he follows his mother out of the den. She moves slowly. She has lost a lot of weight over the winter. It's time to eat!

Baby Bears

Baby black bears usually weigh less than a pound at birth.

The cub watches his mother and learns how to find food. He sniffs for ants and grubs. He gobbles up berries and wildflowers.

The mother bear teaches him how to climb a tree. She knows he will be safe there while she hunts for food. The woods are dangerous for cubs. Wolves, mountain lions, and grizzly bears sometimes hunt for little bears. High in the tree, the baby bear snacks on leaves and takes a nap.

Suddenly the mother bear stands up on her hind feet. She smells danger. She growls a warning. The baby bear watches from his perch.

It's a mountain lion! The mountain lion stops when he sees the mother bear towering over him, ready to fight. He runs away.

Little Bears

Baby bears weigh 4 to 8 pounds (1.8 to 3.6 kilograms) when they leave their den in the spring.

All summer and fall, the mother bear and her cub walk through the forests, eating as much as they can. They must gain weight to survive winter. As the weather turns cold, the mother bear looks for a new den for them to spend winter. She spots the perfect place—a cave with a narrow opening.

The mother bear and her cub prepare the den by laying down **moss** and leaves for their beds. Then they snuggle together and begin their long rest.

When spring arrives, the cub is almost fully grown. He will stay with his mother for a little longer, and then, as all bears do, he will wander off to a different part of the woods.

Bear Beds

Many black bears prefer to sleep on soft beds for winter. The bears build their beds by bringing grass, leaves, moss, and bark into their dens.

The Body of a Bear

Ghost Bear

One rare kind of black bear has white or cream-colored fur. It lives off the coast of British Columbia in Canada. It is not a polar bear. Native Americans named this bear "spirit bear." Today it is known as a Kermode bear.

Which Bear?

The most common types of bears are black bears and brown bears. It isn't always easy to tell them apart. Not all black bears are black, and not all brown bears are brown! Black bears can be black, brown, reddish, tan, or even white. Some have a patch of white fur on their chests.

Brown bears, including grizzlies, are usually brown, but the color of their fur ranges from tan to black. Grizzly bear fur is light at the end of each hair, which gives these bears a "grizzled" appearance.

Old Fur, New Fur

All bears shed their fur— called **molting**—once a year when their new fur grows in for the winter.

So how do you tell the difference between black and brown bears? One way is by their size. Brown bears are bigger and have a hump on their shoulders. Their ears are short, round, and smaller than the ears of black bears. A brown bear's claws are longer and a lighter color than those of black bears.

On the Move

Bears may look slow, but they can run as fast as 30 miles (48 kilometers) per hour for short distances. That's faster than the fastest human sprinter!

Bears usually walk on all fours, but they can stand on their back feet. Bears stand up to reach food, see into the distance, fight off an attacker, or sniff the air.

Bears spend a lot of time looking for food, a mate, or a place to **hibernate**. They will return to places where they found food in the past.

Strong Swimmers

Bears are good swimmers. They go into the water to catch fish, cool off, escape pesky insects or a **predator**, and sometimes just for fun. Polar bears are the best bear swimmers. They can swim for hours. Black bears can swim a mile (1.6 km) at a time without stopping.

Early Risers

Bears are most active in the early morning and evening. During summer and early fall, when they are storing up fat, bears may be active all day.

Despite their size, bears can run downhill, uphill, and sideways.

Just like people, bears walk by putting their whole foot flat on the ground, heel first.

Paws and Claws

Bear claws are curved. Bears use their claws to turn over rocks and logs, pick berries from bushes, catch fish, and dig up roots. The claws of black bears are so curved that they are able to open the lids of jars!

Sense of Smell

Most bears have good eyesight and hearing, but their sense of smell is the strongest. Bears can sniff out tiny insects inside logs or a dead animal a mile away! A bear's sense of smell is even better than that of a bloodhound.

Bears also use their sense of smell to communicate. They leave their **scent** on trees and bushes to "tell" other bears they are in the area.

Climbing Trees

Black bears learn to climb trees when they are young. Trees offer food (fruit, sweet sap, and insects), safety, and branches for resting. Some bears hibernate in the crook of a branch for the whole winter!

Adult grizzly bears don't climb trees, because they are too big and heavy, but their cubs do.

A black bear climbs by digging into a tree trunk with its front paws and pushing up with its hind legs. It climbs down backward, hind legs first, the way humans do. Bears also slide down tree trunks or jump from low branches.

Smart Bears

Most bears are curious and intelligent. Bears investigate new objects, noises, and smells. They even outsmart humans who try to keep them away from food in garbage cans and at campsites!

Bears have good memories. They can find their way back to places where they have found food—even places they have visited only once before. They remember paths and routes they've walked in the past.

Shy Bears

Both black bears and brown bears are easily scared and shy. However, black and brown mother bears are known for being fierce if their cubs are in danger.

Most brown bears avoid contact with people as much as they can.

Bears make many noises, including grunting, blowing, woofing, and growling. Cubs whine or cry when they are upset or "chuckle" when they are happy.

Chapter 3
Hungry as a Bear

Bear Teeth

Bears have 42 teeth. Humans have 32. A bear's teeth are shaped for eating both plants and animals. The pointed front teeth hold food, such as a wriggly fish, while the bear's flat **molars** work like yours for crushing and grinding.

Bears eat mostly plants, but they love fish. Grizzlies will wait at rivers to catch salmon. Brown bears can eat up to 90 pounds (41 kg) of salmon a day!

Lunchtime All the Time!

Scientists classify bears as **carnivores**, or "meat-eating" animals. However, bears are actually **omnivores**. They eat both plants and animals. In fact, mostly they eat plants.

Bears eat practically anything, but their favorite foods are fruit, nuts, acorns, and insects. They also eat fish, small **mammals**, and honey. In some areas, brown bears hunt larger animals such as moose, elk, and mountain goats. The type of food that bears eat varies, depending on where they live and the time of year.

Bears spend most of spring, summer, and fall searching for food in order to store fat for winter hibernation.

Berry Picking

Black bears can pick berries one at a time from bushes! They pull off the berries with their lips. They also use their claws.

Ready for Winter

Bears are masters of survival. They have developed a perfect way to **conserve** energy during winter, when food is scarce. How do they do this? They hibernate, or sleep, through the winter.

Bears hibernate in dens, which they begin to get ready in September or October. Bears choose many different kinds of places to build their dens, including caves, holes in the ground, or hollow logs. Sometimes they make their dens high up in a tree.

Some bears use the same den every winter. Others choose a new one every year.

During late summer and early fall, bears gain weight to get ready for winter. They eat as much as they can, day and night. Depending on the amount of food available, black bears at this time of year may gain 6 pounds (2.7 kg) a day. The extra fat feeds the bears during winter and helps keep them warm. As cold weather approaches, bears stop eating and grow tired and sleepy.

Warm-weather Bears

Black bears that live in Florida and other southern states don't usually hibernate. But they often make a den and sleep for periods of a few days during winter. Pregnant female black bears will hibernate in winter months.

Bears that hibernate in winter sometimes wake up and leave their dens for a little while to look for food.

A bear that sleeps through winter needs only half the amount of oxygen it needs when it's awake and active.

The Big Sleep

In cold climates, bears sleep in their dens for as long as seven months—usually from mid-September to mid-April. The colder the winter, the longer bears sleep. They do not eat, drink, or get rid of waste during this time. Sometimes bears wake up and come out of their dens, but they come back and go to sleep again.

During hibernation, bears live off the body fat they stored before winter. When the weather warms up, usually in April or May, the bears come out of their dens. At first they are weak. They have lost as much as half their body weight. But as plants grow, the bears begin to eat and gain weight again. Then their energy returns.

A Long Winter's Nap

Some scientists believe that bears are not true hibernators. Their body temperature and heart rates do not drop greatly like those of other animals, such as ground squirrels and chipmunks.

Chapter 4
Bears and Babies

Mother bears teach their cubs how to find food and how to escape from predators. They are very protective of their little ones and will attack if their cubs are in danger.

Mother Bears

Female black bears are ready to have babies when they are about five years old. They give birth to cubs every two or three years. Bears mate in May or June. The baby bear, however, does not begin to grow inside its mother until she has begun to hibernate, usually around November. Then it grows quickly. The bear cub is usually born in January or February, while the mother is hibernating. A mother bear usually gives birth to one to three cubs at a time, but scientists have recorded as many as six born to one mother.

Baby Bears Need Their Moms!

At birth, baby bears are tiny, toothless, and covered with wispy fur. They cannot see, hear, or smell until they are older. Baby bears are able to walk when they are five or six weeks old.

Baby Bears

When a mother bear gives birth, she licks her cubs and keeps them close to her. Once they begin to **nurse**, she falls back into her deep sleep. The cubs eat and sleep for two to three months. The mother bear's milk is high in fat. The babies grow quickly.

As soon as the cubs come out of the den, the mother bear teaches them to find food. She shows them how to climb trees and rescues them from any danger by carrying them in her mouth. In fall of the cubs' first year, mother and cubs prepare a den. They sleep together until spring.

Not long after the cubs leave the den for the second time, when they are about 17 months old, they are ready to leave their mother. She may recognize her **offspring** for years to come and allow them to search for food in her territory.

Bear Play

Bear cubs are playful. They climb trees, wrestle, play fight, and chase each other. Playing helps make them strong. Playing also gives cubs the social skills they need. By learning to understand other bears' behavior, cubs will be ready to know if a strange bear is friendly or not.

Bear cubs like to climb on their mother's back for fun, comfort, or a better view!

Chapter 5
Bears in the World

39

Are Koalas Really Bears?

Koalas look like bears. Many people refer to them as koala bears. But koalas are not bears! They are members of a special group of mammals called **marsupials**. Marsupial moms have a built-in pouch for carrying their babies. Can you think of another marsupial that has a pouch? If you thought of a kangaroo, you are right!

Polar bear cubs stay with their mothers until they are two years old.

All Kinds of Bears

There are many kinds of bears that live in different places around the world.

- **Black bears** and **brown bears** live in North America. Some brown bears live in Europe.

- **Polar bears** live where the climate is very cold—in the **Arctic**. They are the best swimmers of all the bears.

- **Spectacled bears** get their name from the circles around their eyes that look like spectacles (eyeglasses). These bears live in the Andes Mountains in South America.

- **Sloth bears** live in tropical and subtropical forests of India and Sri Lanka. They are slow movers.

- **Sun bears** live in tropical and subtropical forests of Southeast Asia.

- **Panda bears** live in China. They eat leaves from bamboo trees.

Bear Homes

Black bears and brown bears mostly live in forests. A bear's territory is often made of smaller areas linked by paths. Within its home range, a bear can travel to different **habitats**—from berry patches to rivers with salmon.

Fast Facts About Bears

	Black Bear	Grizzly Bear
Scientific Name	*Ursus Americanus*	*Ursus arctos horribilis*
Order	Carnivora	Carnivora
Family	Ursidae	Ursidae
Size	Male 5–6 feet (1.5 to 1.8 m) tall	Male 5–8 feet (1.5 to 2.5 m) tall
Weight	Females average 150 pounds (68 kg); males average about 285 pounds (129 kg)	Females range from 200 to 400 pounds (91 to 181 kg); males range from 300 to 850 pounds (136 to 386 kg)
Life Span	Up to 32 years in the wild	25 to 30 years in the wild
Habitat	Forests, woodlands, swamps, mountain forests, tundra	Forests, woodlands, swamps, mountain forests, tundra

The Future of Bears

Black bears and brown bears are not **endangered**, but other bears are, especially giant pandas. The habitats of all bears are often threatened or shrunk by humans. The Arctic, where polar bears live, is in danger because of **global warming**. Warmer temperatures are melting the sea ice that the polar bears depend on.

The most important way to protect bears is by protecting their habitat.

Glossary

carnivore — a meat-eating animal

conserve — to use carefully, or save

cub — a very young bear

den — a place where a wild animal rests or sleeps

endangered — being a species (a specific type) of plant or animal in danger of extinction

global warming — a rise in the average temperature of the Earth's atmosphere that causes a change in climate

habitat — the natural environment where an animal or plant lives

hibernate — to go into a deep sleep for a period of time

mammal — an animal with a backbone and hair on its body that drinks milk from its mother when it is young

marsupial — a kind of mammal whose mother carries her babies in a pouch

molars — big teeth in the back of the mouth used for grinding food

molt — to shed old fur, hair, or skin and have new fur, hair, or skin grow in

moss — a small green plant that forms a soft mat on moist ground, rocks, or trees

nurse — to feed a baby with milk from the mother's breast

offspring — young animals from the same mother

omnivore — an animal that eats both plants and meat

predator — an animal that hunts and eats other animals to survive

scent — a smell left by an animal that other animals can identify

tundra — a big area of land in the Arctic region with no trees and a permanently frozen layer of soil

Bears: Show What You Know

How much have you learned about bears? Grab a piece of paper and a pencil and write your answers down.

1. How much do black bears usually weigh at birth?

2. Which type of bear is the best swimmer?

3. Why do bears leave their scent on trees?

4. How many teeth do bears have?

5. How do bears conserve energy during cold winters?

6. At what age are female black bears ready to have babies?

7. Where do spectacled bears live?

8. Which type of bear lives in India and Sri Lanka?

9. How long can a black bear live in the wild?

10. Why is the polar bear's habitat in danger?

1. Less than a pound 2. The polar bear 3. To tell other bears they are in the area 4. 42 5. By hibernating 6. At about 5 years old 7. In the Andes Mountains of South America 8. The sun bear 9. Up to 32 years 10. Because of global warming

For More Information

Books

Black Bear: North America's Bear. Swinburne, Stephen R. (Boyds Mills Press, 2003)

Ice Bear: In the Steps of the Polar Bear. Davies, Nicola (Candlewick, 2005)

Searching for Grizzlies. Hirschi, Ron (Boyds Mills Press, 2005)

Web Sites

National Geographic Kids

www.kids.nationalgeographic.com/Animals/CreatureFeature/Brown-bear

Learn all about brown bears and check out lots of fun activities, including videos and quizzes.

North American Bear Center

www.bear.org/website

Find facts about bears, and learn how to protect their habitats. Check out the bear sighting map!

Publisher's note to educators and parents: Our editors have carefully reviewed these web sites to ensure that they are suitable for children. Many web sites change frequently, however, and we cannot guarantee that a site's future contents will continue to meet our high standards of quality and educational value. Be advised that children should be closely supervised whenever they access the Internet.

7292

Index